LIFE SKILLS

RAISING money

Barbara Hollander

Heinemann LIBRARY

www.heinemann.co.uk/library
Visit our website to find out more information about **Heinemann Library** books.

To order:

 Phone 44 (0) 1865 888066

 Send a fax to 44 (0) 1865 314091

 Visit the Heinemann Bookshop at www.heinemann.co.uk/library to browse our catalogue and order online.

Heinemann Library is an imprint of **Pearson Education Limited**, a company incorporated in England and Wales having its registered office at Edinburgh Gate, Harlow, Essex, CM20 2JE. Registered company number: 00872828

"Heinemann" is a registered trademark of Pearson Education Limited.

Text © Pearson Education Limited 2009
First published in hardback in 2009
The moral rights of the proprietor have been asserted.

Editorial: Megan Cotugno and Harriet Milles
Design: Philippa Jenkins
Production: Alison Parsons
Picture Research: Liz Alexander
Originated by Modern Age Repro House Ltd.
Printed and bound in China by South China Printing Company Ltd.

ISBN 978 0 43111235 0 (hardback)
13 12 11 10 09
10 9 8 7 6 5 4 3 2 1

British Library Cataloguing-in-Publication Data
Hollander, Barbara
   Raising money. - (Life skills)
   1. Fund raising - Juvenile literature
   I. Title
   361.7'0681
A full catalogue record for this book is available from the British Library.

Acknowledegments
We would like to thank the following for permission to reproduce photographs:
©Alamy pp. **43** (iklimfotostock), **21** (Jim West), **25** (StormStudio); ©Corbis pp. **30** (Flint), **15** (Virgo Productions/Zefa), **37** (Tom Stewart); ©Dreamstime.com/Logoboom p. **33**; ©Getty Images pp. **49** (Dave Hogan), **4** (Hulton Archive/ Blank Archives), **34** (Iconica/PM Images), **7** (Spencer Platt); ©PA Photos/AP Photo pp. **40** (Detroit Free Press/Amy Leang), **27** (News & Record/Jerry Wolford), **28** (The Herald-Sun/ Beth Ely); ©Rex Features/Tony Kyriacou p. **18**; ©Roy Ooms/Masterfile.com p. **16**; ©Topham Picturepoint/Ellen Senisi /The Image Works p. **11**; ©UNICEF p. **9**.

Cover photograph of man with a bonsai tree reproduced with permission of © Punchstock/ Digital Vision.

The publisher would like to thank Tristan Boyer Binns for her invaluable assistance in the preparation of this book.

Every effort has been made to contact copyright holders of material reproduced in this book. Any omissions will be rectified in subsequent printings if notice is given to the Publishers.

Contents

Some words are printed in bold, **like this**. You can find out
what they mean by looking in the glossary.

Why raise money?

In the 1980s, people watched as a crisis developed in Ethiopia, Africa. On the television news people saw pictures of babies, children and families dying because they did not have enough to eat. A lot of people felt they needed to do something to help.

We are the world

In 1985, a group of famous musicians recorded a song called "We are the World". Michael Jackson, Bruce Springsteen, and more than 40 other singers participated. The song and its related **merchandise** raised more than £50 million. Everyone who bought the song helped raise money.

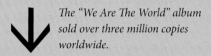

The "We Are The World" album sold over three million copies worldwide.

When people see a problem, they often want to help. But many of these problems are far away, and we can't help directly. What we can do is give money to people who can get the help to where it is needed. Closer to home, it is easier to help directly. If your school needs new books, or your community needs a new playground, you can raise money to help.

Rewarding

Organising fundraising activities can cost you time and energy – but the rewards are great. Stepping outside your own needs and seeing what others need is a big part of growing up. And knowing that your thoughts, efforts, and energy helped to solve a problem is a great feeling.

By raising money for charity, you will learn to recognize and use your own talents and abilities. You will have to set goals, and have the determination to achieve them.

What can raising money do for you?

- It can teach you valuable skills such as organisation, how to advertise, and money management.

- It can strengthen your "people skills" because most fundraising events involve teamwork. This means learning to work alongside other people. You usually have customers too, so you learn to sell to people.

- It can teach you to use your own initiative. You decide on the type of fundraising activity and make other important decisions.

- It can increase your self-confidence, and help you to realise how much you are capable of doing.

- It can improve your self-awareness. Choosing the appropriate fundraising activity is about understanding your talents and interests, finding the best way to use them, and discovering what is important to you.

- It can give you the chance to help others. You can make a real difference in someone's life by raising money for a charity of your choice.

- It can give you a great sense of achievement. It's nice to receive money from an allowance or a birthday present. But being able to donate money you have raised all on your own is an even better feeling!

- Most fundraising events are fun, too!

This book contains useful tips and advice to help you meet your fundraising objectives. It should help you to feel confident about working as part of a group, or about managing it all on your own. By using the right strategies, you will see it is possible to raise quite significant sums of money.

A BIT ABOUT CHARITIES

Human beings are strange creatures. We wage war with each other. We can be very suspicious of other countries and other cultures. But we still hate to watch our fellow human beings suffering. If a disaster happens – either man-made or natural – you can be sure a charity will immediately spring up to help the victims.

CHOOSING A CAUSE

All charities have a specific goal. These goals may include:

- protecting, supporting, and educating children
- feeding the hungry in countries where there is famine
- feeding, clothing, and sheltering refugees or disaster victims
- education for the poor
- protecting the environment
- protecting animal species
- animal welfare
- medical research into cures for life-threatening or disabling diseases and conditions
- supporting people with **chronic** illness or disabilities
- helping victims of war, or war veterans
- helping the elderly
- helping the homeless

Feel committed!

Run your eye down the list on the left. You may feel something's missing. Are there causes you feel strongly about that are not on the list? If so, write these down on a piece of paper.

Thanks to modern technology – television, newspapers, and the Internet – we know much more about local, national, and global issues than our great-grandparents, grandparents, or even our parents. So much so, that it is easy to feel overwhelmed by the amount of information out there. It is easy to end up thinking, "There's so much suffering, I want to support everything!" or, "There's so much suffering and I can do nothing to help!"

Both of these reactions are normal, but unrealistic. You cannot help everyone and solve every problem, but you can pick one cause you feel passionate about and make a difference there. It is very important that the cause you support is one you genuinely care about. Unless you feel truly committed to the cause you are supporting, you won't make a committed or effective fundraiser.

Some large, international charities meet the needs of people around the world. There are also national organisations that help people throughout a country or region. Local charities work within an even smaller area. All these organisations need fundraisers to help them provide this support.

Your efforts matter, even if you raise small amounts of money. By talking about a cause you believe in, you help other people learn about it. You can both raise funds, and spread the word through your work.

The 2004 Asian tsunami was one of the worst natural disasters in history. The millions of pounds raised by charities are helping the survivors to rebuild their shattered lives.

Getting it
Right

Always check out a charity before deciding to support it. Unfortunately some so-called charities are not what they seem. Some people use fundraisers' money to pay themselves or their staff large salaries, instead of giving it to their cause. Ask your parents or teacher to help you research whether a charity is reputable. All charities you donate to should be registered as charities with the government.

INTERNATIONAL AID

International charities allow people to participate in many ways. These organisations make it easy for members to fundraise by giving them ideas, packs, computer sponsorship forms, and email cards. They also sponsor contests intended to raise awareness about their causes. These organisations make helping others easy – and fun!

Do your research

When you have picked the cause you want to support, you can research their fieldwork online. Most of the big international charities have excellent websites. These will tell you details about the organisation's fundraising efforts. You should be able to see what money has been raised, and how it has been spent. The website will also have the charity's **mission** statement. This describes the purpose and vision of the organisation.

Register support

Make sure you have checked out a few possible charities, then pick the one that matches your interests and concerns. You will probably be able to register online as a supporter. If you need any materials, you can ask for them.

Some international charities have local meetings, or local events already organised that you can take part in.

Before you register, give out your address, or plan to go to any events, check with your parents to make sure they agree.

Once you have registered as a supporter, many charities will send you regular updates through the post or by email. You can learn more about their work, and hear about what other fundraisers have been up to.

Worldwide efforts

Being a part of an international team makes a difference. These large organisations involve people all around the world, who raise money in many different ways. An Australian may be raising money by washing cars, while a Canadian may be raising money through a carnival. Yet both individuals are contributing to the same cause, and making a difference by helping others.

"A man who gives to charity in secret is greater than Moses."

(From the Talmud, *the book of Jewish law and tradition.*)

DID YOU KNOW?

The United Nations Children's Fund (UNICEF) is the largest worldwide organisation dedicated to helping children around the world. It provides safe places to live, medical treatment, food, and education to children in need. In 2006, fundraising gave UNICEF more than £175 million to spend on helping children. A lot of that money came in small amounts from individual people or small groups.

UNICEF helps fundraisers by providing:
- sponsorship forms
- sample request letters
- thank-you letters
- sample press releases.

UNICEF will also send out a fundraising folder with materials such as balloons, pins, and pamphlets describing their cause.

One of UNICEF's programmes is Youth Voice. Young people aged 11 to 18 are encouraged to raise money to help kids in need around the world.

Helping your school

All pupils have moments when they just hate school! But take a moment to sit down and think about the opportunities your school has given you, and how valuable it has been in your life.

As well as giving you an education, it has surrounded you with a community of friends. It has given you chances to do things that you might never have done without the encouragement of your teachers and classmates.

All parents, teachers, and pupils want their local schools to be the best they can be – for now and for the future. If you want to make a difference by raising money to support your school, talk to your teachers about where the greatest needs lie.

Locating the need

Does your school library need new books, or better tables and chairs?

Does your school's IT equipment need upgrading?

Maybe your school's sports equipment is outdated?

Perhaps there is a worthwhile school trip that you and your classmates would like to go on?

Could your school improve its learning access for fellow pupils who are visually impaired or have hearing difficulties?

Getting it Right

The pupils of Orwell Park School raised more than £5,000 by holding a fancy dress fun run. They were sponsored by families and friends to run in aid of their chosen charity, Great Ormond Street Hospital for Sick Children, in London. The run was inspired by James Murray, a former patient at the hospital and pupil at the school. He wanted to thank the hospital for the treatment he received. Could your school work together to raise money for an important cause like this?

Most schools have a fairly long "wish-list" of items or services they either desperately need, or would like to improve. Talk to your fellow pupils about the school facilities that you feel could be improved. Talk to the school's parent-teacher association to see what other needs they may know about.

Helping your community

By "community" we mean your neighbourhood – your local area or town, and the people who live in it.

Are the local playgrounds in your community run-down, dirty, or dangerous?

Is there adequate wheelchair access at your local shopping centre?

Do the poor, sick, or elderly people in your neighbourhood need more **amenities** or support?

Maybe your community could do with safer road crossings, or even a garden for local people to enjoy?

Do your local sports facilities need better equipment?

You may have heard your parents, your friends' parents, or local radio stations complaining about local problems that need to be solved. There could be some things about your local area that have been annoying you and your friends for some time.

Well, you don't have to just sit there feeling upset or annoyed about it – you can get out there and do something to help!

Later in this book we will be explaining just how you can put together good ideas for community fundraising, and help to make a real improvement in the lives of others in your community.

Talk to your teachers about ideas you might have for school fundraising.

Fundraising on your own

There are many ways to raise money for charity. Some are best done on your own; some work better with small groups; and some need a really big team behind them to make a success of the project. This chapter has ideas for fundraising on your own.

HARD WORK!

Make no mistake – doing it on your own can be hard work! You will need to stay focused and be hardworking and determined to succeed. You must be prepared to sacrifice time that you might prefer to spend with friends or doing other things (watching television for instance). When raising money on your own, you will be responsible for deciding what to do, how to do it, and when to stop.

However, if you achieve your goal, you will impress your family, your teachers, and perhaps even your future employers. Most importantly, you will impress yourself! That great feeling of having made a real difference to other people's lives is hard to beat.

Staying positive

Raising money all on your own is in many ways a lot tougher than doing it as part of a group. In a group, the load of responsibility is spread among the group members. When you are on your own, you cannot rely on other group members to keep you going when things get difficult. You have to keep yourself motivated. This is another reason why it is so important to feel absolutely committed to the cause you are raising money for.

Fundraising on your own means keeping your attitude positive at all times, and summoning up all your determination and energy. It also means planning your time very carefully. For instance, there will be nobody to stand in for you if you suddenly find you cannot do something on a certain day.

Be realistic

When deciding how you are going to raise money on your own, you need to be very realistic about the things you are good at. Also, think long and hard about the things that you are frankly not much good at, or that would bore you.

You may decide to sell your services, or sell items that you have made.

You could decide to sell things you no longer need. If you want to succeed, it is important to choose the fundraising opportunity that best matches your interests and abilities.

Making connections

So, you've chosen your cause? You're ready? You're determined to succeed? Let's think of the best ways for you to raise money. Here's the plan:

First, list your interests, or the things you like to do. Then list the things you are good at, or your abilities. Be honest with yourself – but try not to be too hard on yourself either!

Everyone has interests and abilities, even if they think they don't. If you are feeling stuck, try asking your friends what they think your abilities are. You might be quite surprised by what they say!

Now look for connections between your interests and abilities, to find the best ways for you to raise money. Below are some simple examples. Your interests or abilities may not be on this list. If that is the case, just add them in! Then think of projects that would best suit you.

Interest	Ability
Films	Schoolwork
Listening to music	Playing an instrument
Animals	Being a good friend
Shopping	Working with children
House design	Assembling things
Reading books	Sport
Art projects	Being creative
Plants and flowers	Organisation
Sport	Cooking

Now match your interests with your abilities to discover some fundraising opportunities

Interests and abilities	Fundraising projects
Art projects/being creative	Face painting
Listening to music/playing an instrument	Music lessons or performing
Animals/sport	Walking dogs
Shopping/being creative	Gift wrapping
Reading books/working with children	Babysitting
Art projects/assembling things	Making jewellery
Plants and flowers/sport	Mowing lawns, gardening
House design/organisation	Cleaning jobs, home decorating

SPECIAL EVENTS

When raising money, remember that there are certain times of year when people have particular reasons for spending extra money – such as Christmas and Easter. At these times, people often like to know that some of the extra money they spend on presents, special food, or extra help is going to a good cause. The good fundraiser will be aware of these particular needs, and ready to meet them.

In the table below are a few examples of how you can match goods and services to special events. You can probably think of many other festivals and holidays where special presents or services would be welcomed, and would sell well. For example, Chinese New Year, Diwali, and Ramadan. Do your research, and think about ways in which you could meet people's particular needs at particular times of year. Be creative!

Event	Goods or services
Christmas	Cards, presents, wrapping paper, baking, carol singing, making tree decorations, babysitting
Easter	Cards, baking, painted eggs, making chocolates and sweets, growing Spring bulbs in pots

Matching needs

It is important to be aware of the needs of your family, friends, and community. These needs will create a demand for a product or service. Good fundraisers understand the needs of those around them. They match these needs to their interests and abilities.

If you like to be outdoors, think of the seasons. What particular needs (and fundraising opportunities) does each season bring in your local community?

- *Spring*: people like to plant out flowers in spring. Maybe you could grow flowers or herbs from seed and sell them locally?

- *Summer*: grass grows fast in the summer. You could make money by mowing lawns. Picking fruit and washing cars are also good summer earners.

- *Autumn*: clearing fallen leaves is a good job for the autumn. Late fruit-picking is also an option.

- *Winter*: clearing snow and ice and gritting pathways are good jobs for winter. Also clearing gardens of late autumn debris.

Getting it Right

Maria wanted to raise money for her local hospital. The Christmas holidays were fast approaching. First Maria made a list of ways to raise money by combining her interests and abilities. Then she made another list of the likely needs of her family, friends, and community in the Christmas period.

Ideas to raise money	People's holiday needs
Making cards	Extra housework
Walking dogs	Christmas presents
Gift wrapping	Christmas cards
Babysitting	Special foods
Making jewellery	Childcare

Maria knew that around Christmas time there would be more demand for gift wrapping than for dog walking. Busy mums and dads would also welcome extra childcare at this busy time, and help with baking and cooking special foods.

Gift wrapping is a fun and creative way to raise money at Christmas.

PLAN SAFE

Planning your own fundraising activity can be rewarding and good fun. However, there are a few golden rules that young people should be aware of before starting out:

- NEVER make door-to-door calls on your own. Always make sure you have at least one friend or a responsible adult with you.

- NEVER go into a stranger's house without first telling your parents where you are – the name of the householder, and their address.

- NEVER give people your own address or telephone number unless you are absolutely certain that they are 100 percent trustworthy.

- If you secure a job over the telephone – say, babysitting or lawn mowing – always say that you need to get your parents'

permission first, before agreeing to start work.

- NEVER agree to walk a dog that is aggressive, or that scares you. Get to know the dog before you take it out. Make sure the dog's leash and collar are strong, and that it wears a muzzle if appropriate.

- NEVER agree to babysit a child that has an infectious disease. An unwell child needs to be cared for by its parents or a responsible adult.

- If you are running a stall, be sure to keep a careful eye on the money you make. Take along a secure container to keep it in, and never leave it unattended. Try to take a friend along to help you with this. Unfortunately there are some people out there who would love to pocket your hard-earned funds!

If you like animals, and you are strong and healthy and prefer to be outdoors, dog walking is a good way to raise money. But make sure you don't take on more than you can handle!

• CHECKLIST •

Top individual fundraising ideas

- Cake sales
- Lemonade stall
- Lawn mowing
- Gift wrapping
- Making greetings cards
- Making jewellery
- Babysitting
- Sponsored run, walk, swim, or read
- Dog walking
- Pavement sale (sell unwanted items by clearing out your cupboards)
- Bingo night
- Quiz night
- Distributing leaflets
- Car cleaning

DID YOU KNOW?

Ben Johnson was 14 years old when his brother Tristan died of leukaemia, a type of cancer. Ben's experiences as the sibling of a seriously ill child, and the feelings he faced after Tristan died, left him feeling in need of help. He joined up with a friend, whose sister had also died of cancer, and together they started up a new charity called Siblinks.

The charity aims to support young people aged 13–25 years old who have had a sibling or other family member affected by cancer. It provides a network for young people who are going through this experience, to give them support through social, practical, and emotional activities, and to provide information and raise awareness. It organises weekends away for its members, and has set up an email network where young people can share their feelings without giving away too much personal information.

Ben's story shows how individuals can make a difference by helping to meet the needs of others.

Raising money with a group

Working in teams has many benefits, including sharing responsibilities and using the combined interests and strengths of team members. If you're happy to commit to working with other people to raise money, there are a lot of ways you can do it.

Joining in

You can join in an existing group or activity, such as a charity fun run or a read-a-thon. You can decide to start your own group or activity, and set up the team to run it. It's easiest to join in something someone else has organised. Some of the big international charities promote coffee mornings, **sponsored** walks, or other group activities. You simply register as a contributor, then carry out the activity. Your school may have an annual school fair, and you can help by donating your time or old toys and books for a stall.

This group of students staged a "gorilla-thon" to raise money for victims of breast cancer – and they clearly had a lot of fun along the way!

DID YOU KNOW?

A sponsor is someone who agrees to **donate** money to your cause on your behalf. You ask sponsors to make **pledges** of money when you finish the walk, or for every book you read, or when you reach your goal. You have to collect the money from the sponsors when the event is over.

If you need to organise an activity with a group you may be able find some ideas in this table. There will be more ideas later in the book.

Group fundraising ideas	
Cake sale	Arrange for people to make cakes, biscuits, and brownies and sell them to raise money.
Car wash	Good weather makes car washing a fun choice. All you need are buckets of water, soap, and lots of dirty cars. Charge a price for each car you wash. Remember that location is key – choose a safe but busy spot, where many drivers will see you.
Talent show	Gather a talented group of people and sell tickets to watch them perform.
Concert	Schools, local bands, and even professional singers can give fundraising concerts. Asking professional musicians to donate their services will lower the event's costs.
Contest	Be creative! Types of fundraising contests include singing, fancy dress, dog shows, and funniest photos or videos.
Sports	Football tournaments, basketball games, and sponsored runs and swims can turn a friendly competition into a great fundraising event.
Class or school cookbook	Collect favourite recipes from friends, teachers, parents, and relatives and make them into a book to sell to everyone you know.
Fête or fair	Fairs with prizes, games, and food can be popular events. The more people who attend, the more money you make. You can charge an entrance fee, as well as a fee to participate in the different activities.

JOINING A COMMITTEE

If you want to make new friends, develop leadership skills, or help an organisation you already belong to, joining a committee can be a great way to do all these things – and many more!

Look for sign-up sheets at school. A fundraising event run by the student council often encourages participation from all pupils. You can also ask around – talk to parents, teachers, and friends about the organisations in your school and community.

The committee

Most groups have a **committee** to run them. This is a small team that represents or makes decisions for the whole group. Most committees have a **chairperson**, a **secretary**, and a **treasurer**.

- The chairperson makes an **agenda**, runs the meetings, and is the voice of the group.

- The secretary takes **minutes**, and is the "pen" of the group, writing letters and making phone calls.

- The treasurer runs the accounts. The accounts are records of all the group's income and expenses. If your group is big enough for a bank account, the treasurer is responsible for that, too. He or she will write and deposit cheques.

Division of labour

The committee in charge of an event usually makes decisions about the **division of labour**. The group breaks down the event into jobs and assigns jobs to different people. This division of labour allows many people to help in different ways and to accomplish the job together.

Getting it Wrong

Don't think you can run a group all by yourself. You need people with other talents to make your team a success. If you're thinking big, you need lots of people's energy and help to meet your goals. Don't exclude people or try to keep all the power to yourself! Working as part of a committee also provides a safety net. If one member has difficulty completing a job, he or she can ask another member for help.

It can be fun to work as part of a committee, especially when you raise a lot of money and get big things done!

The ideal committee

An ideal committee would be made up of the following people:

- Someone with good leadership skills – but not too "bossy"! This person would make a good chairperson.

- Someone who is good at maths. This person would make an ideal treasurer.

- Someone who has good organisational skills. This person would make a good secretary.

- Someone who has creative or artistic flair. This person would be great at designing **publicity** material and thinking of original and creative ideas.

- Someone who is good at talking, persuading, and getting their ideas across. This person could be good at sales and publicity.

- Some hardworking, energetic people who are committed to the fundraising venture.

STARTING YOUR OWN COMMITTEE

Sometimes you need to start your own group to raise money. Here's how to get that going.

First, decide on a name that explains what the project is. For instance, if you want to build a new playground on Broad Street, you could call yourselves The Broad Street Playground Project. Then advertise for other people to join you. You could put up posters at school or in your community, send out emails to friends, and call people you know to see if they'd like to help.

Think about your friends. Do any of them have some of the qualities listed on the previous page. Would they like to join the committee with you – or help you form a committee of your own? Your friends might know of other people who would make good committee members.

Listen to your group

Once you have a group of people, it is time to call your first meeting. Talk through the fundraising project. Ask individual members about their ideas for fundraising, what tasks they think they would do best, and what they would most enjoy doing. Take a little time to listen to the group talk through ideas amongst themselves. This sometimes makes it easier to spot the person who would be best for a particular role.

Once these decisions have been made, you can form your committee – and you're ready to get going!

• CHECKLIST •

Here are some questions to ask yourself before you start to form a committee:

- Who will be on the committee? Find a group of peers who want to raise money for the same cause.

- Is there an adult helping the committee? A teacher or a parent can provide supervision and help with activities that require an adult. For instance, you may need an adult to drive the group around or to make a cash deposit (put down money) to reserve a location for an event.

- Why are you making money? Outline your goals. Is everyone in agreement about them?

- How can you use division of labour to organise and carry out the event?

ARE YOU A TEAM PLAYER?

1) Your teacher gives the class a big history project and divides everyone into groups. You:
a) do your part of the assignment.
b) call a meeting to switch parts.
c) write the whole report yourself.

2) The P.E. teacher lets the class decide how to spend its time. You:
a) join a basketball game.
b) join a football game.
c) run on the track by yourself.

3) You have just learned that some children in your country have never had a holiday in their lives. You want to raise money to help them. You:
a) get your friends together to plan a fundraising event.
b) ask your school to get involved.
c) raise the money yourself by babysitting or washing cars.

4) Your friend talks you into joining a school club. The club wants to raise money for a trip that sounds like fun. You:
a) volunteer to be the committee's leader.
b) get together with your friend to make leaflets and posters.
c) ask your parents or guardians for a donation.

5) Your community is running a card design fundraising event. A lot of your friends are signing up. You:
a) join your friends for a meeting.
b) ask your parents how you can do your part.
c) design cards and sell them on your own, then donate the money that you raised to the community.

See answers on page 50.

Running a fundraising event

Whatever kind of fundraising event you choose to run, your group will need to be highly organised to make it a success.

1. PICK AN ACTIVITY

There are so many fundraising activities it can be confusing to know which one to pick. Look at the cause you are raising money for. Some organisations already have pre-planned activities Others leave it to the fundraisers to come up with their own ideas.

Try to think of an activity related to your cause. If you want to help fund a dogs' home, perhaps a sponsored dog walk, or a dog show would work? If you are raising money for UNICEF, try face painting for children. There are many more suggestions later in this book.

Brainstorming is a good way to come up with a list of ideas. As the ideas come to you, simply write them down or type them on the computer. Do not judge whether the ideas are good or bad – just list them. Later, go back and see which ones are realistic, and which ones are too crazy to succeed.

When you have made a shortlist of activities, you can use research to decide which one will work best for your group. Pick an activity that suits your committee members' interests and strengths. For instance, a cooking club that wants to raise money can hold a cake sale.

Getting it Right

When you set a fundraising goal, make sure it is possible to reach it. Don't be over-ambitious and say you want to raise millions of pounds to buy a new hospital scanner, or build a whole new community centre in a very short time. Goals that are set too high to reach within a time limit make you sound unreliable. Think about breaking down a big project into smaller chunks, such as raising a few hundred pounds this year, or funding just one part of your main goal.

 Face painting is always popular with young children and is a good fundraising activity.

Questions to ask

Ask yourselves and people around you questions such as:

- Is there a need for this service?
- Do people in my community like to… (attend shows, buy jewellery, dance, etc.)?
- What has worked before? Why?

Make sure you can answer all the How, Why, What, Who, and Where questions in the checklist before you actually begin planning the event.

• CHECKLIST •

Research is an important part of every fundraising event. Thorough research will answer these five questions:

- How will you raise money?
- Why are you raising money?
- What are your responsibilities?
- Who are your sponsors or buyers?
- Where will you raise the money? (In your community? At school?)

2. PLANNING THE EVENT

Planning a fundraising activity is a big undertaking. To be successful, an event must be very well organised. The best way to begin is with a strong framework. If you've done your research and picked your event well, you are ready to move on to the actual organising. Now it's time to think about timing, choosing a location, and allocating tasks.

Timing

Choosing a good date for a fundraising activity is key to getting enough people to attend your event. When picking a date, consider these questions:

- What other local events are scheduled at or around the same time? Avoid scheduling conflicts. Will any other events interfere with the event set-up or conflict with the actual event?

- Consider the amount of time it takes to prepare for the event, and factor in all the jobs that need to be done, from advertising to setting up. How much time will the committee need?

- Is the event associated with a particular time of year (such as Christmas)?

- How is the date likely to be affected by people's schedules? Choosing a date during – or

immediately after – a Bank holiday or a school break may pose a problem. Attendance may be poor because people are away. Or some of your committee members may not be around to help out.

Getting it Wrong

Greg and his friends wanted to raise money for a local hospital. They decided to hold a football tournament and charge each of the teams to participate. The group also decided to charge spectators an entrance fee. With their parents' help, they arranged to hold the event at a local park. When the big day arrived, the football players were disappointed that only a few people turned up to watch. Greg later learned that a local school was holding a fair at the same time, and most families chose to go there. Do your research!

Car washes are good outdoor activities.

Choosing a location

Selecting a location often happens at the same time as choosing a date. When selecting a location, there are many factors to consider.

- What size of location is needed for the event? For example, a fair will require more room than a cake sale. To determine size, think about both the space needed for the event and the estimated number of attendees.

- Is the event connected to a location? A school fundraising activity is usually held in a school.

- Is the desired location available on the chosen date?

- Is it easy for people to get to the event? Holding a community event in another town will not encourage local people to attend.

- Will it cost you to use the location? Many places charge fees for using their facilities.

TIP

Always build in extra days or weeks to the amount of time needed for preparation. For example, if you think that it will take two weeks to plan a car wash, then choose a date two-and-a-half weeks away. Remember, unexpected problems and setbacks can happen, so allow extra time!

- Do you need a **permit** to use the location? (See page 36)

- Does the event need to be outdoors or indoors?

Who does what?

Within a club or group, individual team members also have interests and strengths that are better suited to certain tasks. Sometimes a person with a particular interest or strength may want to step outside his or her comfort zone and try something new.

This can lead to discovering new interests. Both the similarities and the differences among team members make for a successful team.

Take a look at the table below. Now match team members' interests and skills with the most appropriate job.

Interests and skills	Job
1. Writer	A. Keeps checklist
2. Likes art	B. Provides refreshments
3. Family owns an ice cream shop	C. Makes posters
4. Organised person	D. Advertises by email
5. Enjoys working on the computer	E. Writes letters asking for donations

Certain jobs are easier for a group than for one person, such as the setting up and clearing up at events.

Woodbury School

Woodbury School's fundraising committee wants to raise money to buy computers for the school. The committee plans to organise a gifts sale. Local shops that sell products such as books, cards, toiletries, and chocolates will set up stalls at the school. Each vendor has agreed to give a percentage of the money they make to the school. The school can also raise money by charging an entrance fee and by selling refreshments.

Woodbury's fundraising committee needs to complete the following tasks:

- Choosing a date
- Finding a location
- Contacting the vendors
- Writing up **contracts** that specify what percentage vendors will give to the school
- Choosing food and drinks and equipment (cups etc.) for the refreshments stall
- Advertising the event
- Decorating the room
- Collecting entrance fees
- Cleaning up afterwards
- Collecting and accounting for the money raised and spent
- Telling pupils, teachers, and parents how many computers can be bought with the money raised.

The jobs can be shared between the committee's six members:

Member	Job
Sam	Contact vendors
Liz	Arrange for contracts with vendors
Steven	Advertise the event by making posters
Helen	Decorate the room and arrange for the setting up
John	Arrange the refreshment stall
Claire	Collect entrance fees

They can all help with the cleaning up. The committee treasurer can do the accounting, and the chairperson and secretary can tell people about their success.

3. ADVERTISING THE EVENT

Spreading the word about your event is an important part of fundraising. You have to tell people about your fundraising activity so that they can support you. There are several ways to advertise, including:

- *Word of mouth* – tell your family and friends about the event in person or over the phone. Let them know why you are raising money, and the date, time, and place of the event. Ask them to pass on the information to everyone they know.

- *Flyers* – put up posters in your local schools, library, community centres, and shops. Be sure to ask permission before doing this. Many places have noticeboards for announcements.

- *Text* – send a text message to a list of potential guests. Be sure to ask for your parents' or guardians' help and permission.

- *Email* – email is another good way to spread the word to many people at once. A fundraising email can include a description of the event as well as pictures to catch the reader's attention. It can also include a link to the cause associated with the event. Many organisations use email to notify people about fundraising events, ask for donations, and increase their membership.

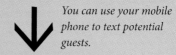

You can use your mobile phone to text potential guests.

4. REMAINING CALM!

When the day of the event arrives, it's easy to get flustered. Even the best-planned events have sudden hitches and crises. The secret to success is to stay calm, even when things seem to fall apart. Usually, the visitors have no idea that things are not going to plan. Keep smiling, keep calm, and be ready to **improvise** – which means to think on your feet!

It's a good idea to make sure all the helpers and planners can be identified during the event. You could have matching T-shirts, or fluorescent vests, or special hats – or simply name badges. This way you can spot each other easily, and the visitors can find you, too.

Another tip is to have a special bag or box full of office supplies, such as blue tack, sticky tape, marker pens, pens, pencils, safety pins, scissors, a stapler, a hole punch, and sticky notes. Most events have sudden, unforeseen needs for these things!

Also ensure you have a first aid kit. Know where the cleaning materials are, and bring whatever other bags and tools you'll need to clear up. Make sure you know what is expected before you leave. Do you need to set an alarm or contact the caretaker?

• CHECKLIST •

A checklist is a good organisational tool on the day. List the things that you have to do in **chronological** (time-related) order. Then tick off the tasks as you complete them. This is an example of a checklist for a school dance-a-thon:

- Sweep floor
- Put up decorations
- Set up refreshment tables
- Set up sound system
- Do a sound check
- Bring in refreshments and lay out
- Set up main gate table
- Give money boxes and change to main gate and refreshment tables
- Make sure adult volunteers are there
- Make sure first aider is there
- Clean up and put everything away afterwards
- Make sure the site is locked and alarmed before going home.

5. Review your event

Soon after your event is over, but not on that same day, have a committee meeting. This is your chance to talk about what worked well, and what didn't. You can make notes for the next time you do something like this. You can find out how much you raised, and what your expenses were. It's very important to take time to thank everyone for their hard work, too.

Getting it Right

A good review meeting agenda might look like this:

1) Presentation by treasurer: **takings**, expenses, and profit.

2) Thank you to the planners and people involved.

3) Agree or review how profit from the event will be spent.

4) Ask everyone around the table to mention something that worked and something that could have gone better.

5) Discuss solutions to any problems that came up.

6) Decide what the group will do next!

Tips for a successful fundraising event:

- Answer the five research questions: How? Why? What? Who? and Where?

- Avoid scheduling conflicts.

- Keep it realistic. Make sure you have reasonable expectations about schedules and timing.

- Teamwork means sharing the work. Give people jobs, and make sure they understand what they are expected to do.

- When working as part of a team, respect your teammates. Do not load people up with more tasks than they can handle.

- Spread the word through word of mouth, print, text messages, and emails.

- Be courteous to customers.

- Use a checklist. This will help you keep track of all the things you have to do to prepare for the event. Put a tick next to completed tasks.

- Call a review meeting and thank all the people who helped you.

6. SPREAD THE WORD – AGAIN!

You will rely on a lot of support from your family, friends, and community to make an event a success. After it's over, the people close to you and the other event planners will know first-hand how it went. But you need to let the rest of your customers know, too. Tell them what you planned, what your goals were, and how well you did in meeting them. Say something about how the event made you feel.

If it was a school event, putting a notice in the newsletter, on the notice board and on the website should spread the word about your success. If it was a community event, think about inviting the local papers to the event and then following up with them afterwards. They may write articles about how well you did. Let the people in your local government know what you did, and why. Who else should know?

DYNAMIC
DANCING DUO
COMPETE FOR COMPUTERS

On 17th June Millbrook School was hopping, as pupils danced to raise money for new computers. The competition was fierce, but one couple was declared the victors – Thomas Smith and Sue Mellon. Sue Mellon said, "I haven't sweated that much in the school gym ever! Not even playing football! It was great to raise so much money, and we had lots of fun." The winners will enjoy a trip for four to a local Wildlife Park. The school's computer fund is now over £500 richer.

Budgeting, licences, and locations

Careful budgeting is the most important factor in successful fundraising. A fundraising event involves expenses and income, so it must have a clear budget.

expenses and income

An expense is an item that costs money. Printing costs for posters and leaflets, or the cost of ingredients for baked goods, are two examples of fundraising expenses.

The income is the money raised from the fundraising activity. Money from selling cakes or raffle tickets, from babysitting or dog walking are all types of income. In order to make money, your income must be greater than your expenses. The amount of money you made minus your expenses is your profit.

Keeping track

It is important to keep careful track of income and expenses associated with a fundraising event. Fundraisers often use computer programs to keep track of income from online sponsors or ticket sales. You can also can use a notebook or a spreadsheet to record income.

When keeping track of expenses, be sure to save receipts and make notes about expenses too small for receipts. It is often the small expeditures that mount up, and catch you out!

Estimating sales

If you are selling a homemade product, you can estimate the number of sales you will make to help determine how many supplies to buy. For example, a person holding a cake sale can estimate the number of cakes he or she will sell, and use this number to determine how many ingredients to buy. But beware! If your estimate of sales is too high, your expenses may end up being greater than your income.

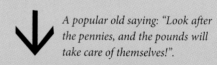

A popular old saying: "Look after the pennies, and the pounds will take care of themselves!".

Dog walking

Richard decided to walk people's dogs to raise money. He kept track of his income and expenses on a spreadsheet.

Week	Income	Expenses	Profit
1	£15	£15 (flyers)	£0
2	£20	£0	£20
3	£30	£0	£30
	Total: £65	Total: £15	Total: £50

In week one, Richard's income was the same as his expenses, so he did not make a profit. But in weeks two and three, Richard made a profit, because in those weeks his income was greater than his expenses. Over the three weeks, Richard raised £50 by walking dogs.

Smart shopping

If you are making items to sell, such as cakes, it pays to shop around for the best deals on ingredients. Perhaps one of your committee members' parents owns a shop or a business, and could supply you with items more cheaply? Or perhaps they could recommend you to other businesses that could help in some way? Remember that you are raising money for a good cause – so be shameless, and just ask! You have nothing to lose, and may have much to gain.

Some shops may offer you a discount on their goods if they know you are raising money for a charity. Shops may even offer you items for free in exchange for asking you to advertise them as a sponsor. In this case, they will give you a notice to put in a prominent position on your stall. This might say something like: "These cakes were made with ingredients kindly donated by Suchandsuch Shop, High Street, Bigtown."

Always ask your parents, guardians, or a teacher before accepting this sort of deal. Also, you should always tell your parents what you are doing, and take some friends or an adult with you when approaching suppliers for possible deals on goods.

Licences

A licence or permit grants government permission to a person or group to run a fundraising activity. Many kinds of event, such as school functions, do not need a licence – but some do.

Rules about licences and fundraising events are different everywhere. It is best to check online or with a local authority to find out your town or city's rules. Applying for a licence involves filling out an application, paying a fee, and following the regulations.

Securing a location

When researching potential locations, pay attention to their costs. Some fundraising locations are offered at no charge, such as school facilities. Others may be rented for a flat fee. Other locations charge per hour, or vary the fee based on the activity that will take place.

If a location charges a fee, you will need an adult to place the deposit (initial payment) and to sign legal documents. It is important to treat the location with respect. Almost all locations will charge extra for any damages caused by the event or the participants.

When selecting a location, be sure to think about size, cost, and accessibility. To calculate the number of hours you need to rent the facility for, include time for setting up and clearing away, as well as the time for the event itself.

HEALTH AND SAFETY REGULATIONS

Be sure to check the health and safety regulations in any location you choose for your event. Certain regulations can make it difficult to hold a big event. For example, you might find that there are strict limits on the number of people you are allowed to have in a venue at any one time. This could be because the access in and out of the building would not be big enough to cope if people needed to get out in a hurry. For example, people could be trapped if a fire broke out.

With a lot people coming and going to a cake sale (for instance) it would be difficult for you to keep track of how many people were in the venue at any one time. You should also consider whether a venue is suitable for people with disabilities.

Flowers are always popular at sales. But remember that your location will need to have a supply of water to keep your flowers fresh – particularly on a hot day. Dead flowers don't sell!

There may also be restrictions that would prevent you from selling certain items – candles for example. And it may not be possible for you to sell certain foods because of health regulations.

For any large function, you should also check whether you need someone with First Aid qualifications to attend, who is able to deal with minor accidents or emergency situations. Ask your teacher or a responsible adult to advise you about how to organise this.

Successful fundraising

Sponsorship can be a very effective way to raise money. Sponsors agree to pay you when you do something special to raise funds for your charity. Some things you can do on your own, such as running a marathon. Others you can do as part of a team, such as crewing in a boat race.

Collecting sponsors

Some people think that sponsorship is a fairly easy way to raise money, but in fact it can be hard work! First, you have to think of people you can approach who might sponsor you; then you have to persuade them to sponsor you; finally, you have to collect the money. And collecting money after the event is often one of the most time-consuming stages.

The key to successful sponsorship is getting a large amount of people to sponsor you. However, the money they promise is no good if it's not collected!

Sponsorship can be raised in various ways. Some of the most popular ways are:

- *Door-to-door* – Take a paper form around your neighbourhood and ask people to sign up. Then collect up the money in cash or cheques after the event.

- *Advertising* – Put up posters advertising the event you are planning (plus a sponsorship form) on your school noticeboard, or other places where people look regularly.

- *Online* – If you are trying to raise money for a large charity, you may find that they have an online system for collecting sponsorship money. The charity will advise you how to go about this.

Door-to-door

When trying to raise sponsorship door-to-door, always remember to take a friend or parent with you on your rounds. You should always carry a clipboard for your sponsorship forms, posters, and so on, and a good supply of pens.

People will need to know that you are **genuine** – meaning that you really are who you say you are, and that you are raising money for a real cause. You should therefore also carry a) some form of identification, and b) something that clearly states the cause you are trying to raise money for.

TO WHOM IT MAY CONCERN:

This is to verify that Jim Brown is a pupil at High Vale School, and he is collecting sponsorship to raise money for our African Schools' project. We hope that you can see your way to support this cause by sponsoring Jim to take part in a 6-mile marathon on 16 April 2009. If you would like to know more about this project, or if you have any concerns or queries, please contact the High Vale School secretary on (telephone number).

Sincerely

(Signature of school staff member)

If you are trying to raise money for your school, it helps to carry a "support letter" from the event organiser or a teacher at your school, stating that the school is supporting your efforts. The letter might read something like the sample above:

Always be polite when householders answer the door to you. Show them your identification and support letter, or any other supporting documents. Explain why you feel committed to the cause, the amount of money that your cause needs to raise, and the event you plan to take part in. Then ask them if they would be prepared to sponsor you.

If they agree, hand them your clipboard with your sponsorship form. This should be divided into four columns (see example below). Ask your sponsors to write down their name, address, and telephone number (if they are happy to give this to you), the amount they would like to donate, and their signature and the date.

When you have collected as many sponsors as possible before the event, take a photocopy of your sponsorship form(s) as a back-up. It would be unfortunate to lose all your sponsors' addresses and pledges!

Jim Brown will be running a 6-mile marathon on 16 April 2009, in aid of the High Vale School's African School's project. Jim is grateful to the following sponsors for their money pledges. The money will be collected on or around 20 April 2009:

NAME	ADDRESS/TEL	AMOUNT	SIGNATURE/DATE
Helen Brook	43 Boundary Road, Newtown NT6 3RH	£1.00 per mile	Helen Brook 26/3/09

FUNDRAISING ONLINE

Large national or international charities will often advertise fundraising events on their websites. These websites will give you the option to either register to take part in an event, or to sponsor someone taking part in the event.

If you want to take part in any large charity event that involves walking, running, or other kinds of sporting activity, you will usually have to agree to a **waiver**. A waiver is an agreement that you will not hold the charity event organisers responsible if you are injured during the event. You will need to get permission from your parents before clicking the "waiver button" online and agreeing to the conditions.

Tips for online success:

- Form a team with friends. If you have a strong team identity, you'll find it easier to get sponsors.

- Decide on an amount as a goal. Aim high but make sure you are realistic!

- Make sure people know how to pay their sponsorship money. Most events have a website where pledges can be paid online.

- If pledges are paid online, you'll be able to keep a check on how close you are to reaching your target.

Taking part in a huge event can be very exciting. Make sure your team stands out from the crowd, so your sponsors will be able to cheer you on.

LETTER CAMPAIGNS

Individuals, school clubs, and many organisations use **letter campaigns** to raise money. These campaigns involve sending out letters to potential donors. Letters can be sent to a large number of people, or to specific members of a community. They also can be sent to a very limited group, such as family and friends. Today many groups send letters via email instead.

If you are planning a letter campaign through the post, remember that you will need to cover the cost of postage and stationery.

Writing a fundraising letter

1) Always begin with a polite heading, such as "To whom it may concern" or "Dear neighbour." Or better still, address to neighbours personally.

2) Describe the fundraising cause. Be sure to answer these questions: Why are you raising money? Who benefits from the money that is being raised? Is there a website that gives more information?

3) Include an address where someone can send a donation. Some organisations include self-addressed, stamped envelopes.

4) Thank potential supporters.

Dear Neighbour,

Have you ever played an instrument? The Victoria School Orchestra is full of pupils like me who love to play instruments. We practise every day at school and give three concerts a year.

We would like to give a concert in a special needs school in the next town on the evening of 20 February 2009. We need to hire a bus that is big enough for all the members of the orchestra. We also need four more music stands for some new orchestra members. The total cost of these items is £500.

Please help us to hire a bus and pay for the music stands. All donations are appreciated. Cheques should be made payable to Victoria School and sent to:

Victoria School Orchestra
124 Bathurst Street
Newtown NT6 7RP

Thank you for your support.

Sincerely,

Alison Jenkins

ORGANISING A RAFFLE

Many fundraising events involve a **raffle**. In a raffle, people buy tickets for a chance to win donated prizes. The money that is raised through ticket sales goes to benefit the group or cause. Committees often plan a raffle as part of a larger event. Charity dinners, lunches, fairs, and gift sales often feature raffles.

Steps for planning a raffle

1) Pick a time and place for the raffle. Most raffles take place during a fundraising event because the high attendance at the event can mean more raffle ticket sales.

2) Make a list of people who might be willing to donate prizes. Prizes can be goods, gift certificates, or services. Many large organisations offer cars, holidays, electronic equipment, and cash as raffle prizes. Think of your family, friends, and community. Ask yourself the following questions:

   - Does anyone you know own a business that could donate a prize?

   - Can the local cinema donate a pair of tickets?

   - Can a nearby restaurant donate a certificate for a free meal?

   - Can the neighbourhood health club donate a month-long membership?

3) Decide on a price for the raffle tickets. Consider your fundraising goal and the cost of the event. Estimate the number of tickets to be sold and choose a reasonable ticket price. Often raffle tickets cost about £1.

4) Get the raffle tickets. You can order them online or buy them in good stationary shops.

5) Advertise the raffle. If the raffle is part of a larger event, add raffle information to flyers, emails, and your publicity material.

Getting it Wrong

Remember that some places require a licence for holding a raffle. Imagine how you would feel if you had worked hard for weeks getting fabulous prizes donated, and organising where, when, and how, only to find the raffle cannot go ahead because you don't have a licence! So make sure you check out the rules before you start planning your raffle.

6) Sell the raffle tickets. Tickets can be sold both before and during the event.

7) Hold the raffle draw and announce the winners.

8) Thank everyone who donated prizes.

Choose about four or five major prizes to feature on posters and other publicity material. Make sure the raffle is seen as a major event in itself, with big prizes at stake.

Getting it Right

Ask your parents or teachers if they can help you to approach local businesses and ask them to donate eye-catching prizes for your raffle. Remember, it's good publicity for the businesses, too, so they should be glad to be seen to support a good cause!

Grouping several smaller prizes to make a large hamper will make a more desirable prize.

Making greetings cards

When Joshua heard about an earthquake that had devastated part of China, he decided he wanted to help. Joshua liked working on his computer and he had great design software, so he decided to make and sell greetings cards to raise money. First, Joshua found an organisation that was helping the earthquake victims. Then he emailed friends and family and told them about his card business, the cause, and the organisation the money would go to. He asked everyone to spread the word and raise awareness of the disaster. He also contacted the local newspaper to tell them his story.

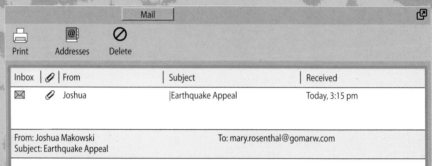

Mail		
Print	Addresses	Delete

Inbox	From	Subject	Received
✉ 📎	Joshua	Earthquake Appeal	Today, 3:15 pm

From: Joshua Makowski
Subject: Earthquake Appeal
To: mary.rosenthal@gomarw.com

Dear Family and Friends,

On 23 January an earthquake devastated part of China. People are struggling to put their lives back together, and I would like to help by raising money for clothes, food, and shelter.

Over the next two weeks, I will be making and selling cards. All the proceeds to benefit the victims of the earthquake will be sent to the charity OXFAM, who are working hard in the earthquake zone. Please support my efforts by wishing someone a happy birthday or anniversary!

Four card designs are attached. All cards are blank inside for your message.

Place your orders online and then pay in person to receive your cards.
Please also tell everyone you know about this disaster, so that more people can help the victims. Thank you for your support.

Joshua

FUNDRAISING HEROES

Hearing stories about other young fundraisers is inspiring. It shows that such actions are appreciated, and encourages others to set up fundraising projects of their own.

Joshua's case study is a good example of someone successfully combining their interests and abilities to raise funds. After their teacher had told the class about an earthquake that had devastated part of China, Joshua returned home and went on the Internet to learn more. He saw pictures of people struggling to survive in an area left in ruins. Joshua wanted to help, so he decided to raise money by using his own talents.

Planning ahead

Joshua enjoyed working on the computer and was fortunate to have design software, a colour printer, coloured ink cartridges, and paper. He decided to go into the card-making business.

Before starting on his fundraising venture, Joshua needed to ask himself some important questions:

- What sort of cards would be likely to sell the best?

- How could he estimate orders so that he did not waste his supplies?

- What would be the most effective way to advertise his cards.?

> *"Never doubt that a small group of thoughtful, committed citizens can change the world; indeed, it's the only thing that ever has."*
>
> Margaret Mead (1901-78), writer and speaker

Joshua's strategy:

1) Find an organisation that helps these earthquake victims. Tell them what he is planning to do.

1) Design four cards – three birthday cards and one general "celebration" card.

2) Send out emails and text messages to family and friends that describe the card business, the cause, and the organisation. Ask them to spread the word.

3) Ask a teacher for advice on how to market the cards at school to raise money for the victims of the earthquake.

5) Contact the local newspaper to see if any reporters are interested in writing about the fundraising story. Give the newspaper his contact information.

6) Take orders and print the cards to fill the orders.

7) Sell the cards and donate the money to the organisation.

Life changing

Taking part in a fundraising campaign, either on your own or as part of a team, will teach you a great deal about yourself. Not only could the experience help to change the lives of others, but it could end up changing your life, too!

Skills for life

Working on any campaign will be a learning experience. Simply by meeting your money-making objectives you will learn a range of valuable life skills. For example:

- How to organise your time efficiently

- How to budget and manage money

- How to interact effectively with others

- How to work on your own initiative or as part of a team

- How to think creatively

- How to sell products or services

To be a successful fundraiser you will need to focus on your abilities and interests, and how best to use them as part of a campaign. In addition, you may get the opportunity to learn some new practical skills, such as graphic design or creative writing (for publicity material), and how to speak well in public. Above all, you may discover surprising new things about yourself – for instance, that you feel very strongly about certain issues.

Not only can fundraising give you the chance to help improve the lives of others (or the planet we live on), and a great sense of personal fulfilment, it can also be great fun!

Can you really make a difference to the world you live in? Of course you can! All it takes is commitment, imagination, determination, and a willingness to work hard. The feeling of achievement you will get after a successful fundraising campaign is hard to beat. So get out there, get raising money – and good luck!

> "You make a living by what you get. You make a life by what you give."
>
> Winston Churchill, British Prime Minister in the 1940s and 1950s

Russell Brand and Lenny Henry promote fundraising fun on Red Nose Day. The celebrity involvement ensures massive media coverage, alongside many opportunities for ordinary people to take part in a wide range of fundraising activities.

DID YOU KNOW?

Some fundraising campaigns have been so successful, they have become annual events:

- The BBC's Children in Need charity works to positively change the lives of disadvantaged children and young people in the UK. Individual fundraisers, schools, and businesses work on thousands of events to raise money. In 2006, Children in Need raised over £33 million. The work of the charity continues throughout the year, but the main event is an annual live show on television featuring some of the fundraising activities taking place, together with entertaining performances from celebrities.

- Comic Relief was first started in the UK in 1985, in response to famine in Africa. It is now an annual fundraising event when famous comedians and entertainers perform for free to raise money for charity. Red Nose Day is an important part of Comic Relief and sales from merchandise (including red noses!) has raised over £174 million since 1988.

Fundraising safely

Fundraising is challenging and fun, but it should also be safe. Whether planning a group fundraising activity or heading out on your own to raise money for your favourite charity, it is important to remember these safety tips:

Make sure your parents or guardians approve. Some fundraising activities may sound good but are not feasible or appropriate. Check with a caregiver before doing an activity, and make yourself well informed so you can discuss it in detail.

Talk to a parent or guardian first. Make a list of potential customers and show it to them – or better still ask them to help you make the list.

Do NOT go to a stranger's house alone when you are selling goods door-to-door, and never enter a stranger's home however persuasive they are. Always take a responsible adult with you. There is safety in numbers when you are selling or delivering products. The other person will know where you are at all times, and can help you out of a difficult situation. They can even help to carry or deliver products!

Carry a mobile phone. Mobile phones make you accessible and can provide help in an emergency.

Do not send out emails or make phone calls to strangers. It is difficult to know whether people online are actually who they say they are. Some people misrepresent themselves (lie about their identity) online. Talking to strangers on the Internet can put you in real danger.

When someone says "I don't have the money right now," do not offer to pay for the fundraising item. A person who wants to borrow money may not pay you back. Remember that you are the seller, not the buyer.

Be honest about the cause you are representing and your fundraising activity. Customers will rely on you for information, such as the date and time of an event. Know your information and relay it accurately.

Do not carry large amounts of cash. Carrying around a lot of cash makes you a target for theft.

ARE YOU SAFETY SMART?

Safety comes first in fundraising. When taking part in an activity, do you know how to play it safe?

1) Your parents are too busy to help you make a list of potential sponsors. You are eager to spread the word, so you:
   a) text your cousins.
   b) open the phone book and start calling random numbers.

2) Your mum gave you permission to visit your next door neighbour to try to fund raise. Your neighbour politely tells you "no" You:
   a) go to the next person on the customer list you agreed.
   b) start going door-to-door.

3) A boy at school tells you that he really wants to buy some of your greetings cards, but he doesn't have the money. The boy asks you to pay now, and he will pay you back later. You do not know this boy, but it would be nice to make another sale. You:
   a) tell the boy, "Sorry, no money, no cards."
   b) lend the boy the money.

4) At your school fundraising event most people paid with money instead of cheques, so you have an envelope full of cash. You:
   a) ask your parent to write you a cheque for the amount of cash you have, then take the cheque to school.
   b) take all the cash to school.

5) The fundraising products have arrived and you want to deliver them. Your brother says he will come with you in an hour. You:
   a) wait for an hour then deliver the products with your brother.
   b) run out and do it by yourself.

6) Your friends think of a way to raise money, but you think project might involve some safety problems. You:
   a) tell the idea to a parent and get their opinion.
   b) go along with it anyway.

See answers on page 50.

QUIZ RESULTS

QUIZ

ARE YOU A TEAM PLAYER?
For page 23

- If most of your answers were a)s and b)s, then welcome to the team.

- If most of your answers were c)s, you clearly prefer working alone. There should be plenty of fundraising opportunities in your local area. Find one that suits you!

QUIZ

ARE YOU SAFETY SMART?
For page 49

- If you answered mostly a)s then congratulations – you play it sensible and safe!

- If most of your answers were b)s you need to develop a better attitude towards safety. Remember that safety must always come first!

20 Things to Remember

1 Believe in the cause that you represent.

2 Belive that you really can make a difference in your school, your community, and the world.

3 Match your interests and talents to find a fundraising activity that's right for you.

4 Remember that raising money can be done in teams or on your own. There's a fundraising activity for everyone.

5 Know that safety comes first. Check with your parents or guardians about fundraising ideas and customer lists.

6 Be courteous to your customers. Treating people with respect earns you a good reputation, so that people will want to support you.

7 When forming a committee, choose teammates that you can trust to be reliable and work hard.

8 Spread the word by word of mouth, flyers, phone calls, e-mails, and text messages.

9 Remember to thank customers, teammates, and donors or sponsors.

10 In a committee, don't try to run the show all on your own. Listen to the views of other committee members and make the best use of their abilities and talents.

11 Learn from mistakes. They are only opportunities to improve!

12 Know that raising money is an accomplishment. Every penny counts.

13 Share the work and the fun. If a fundraising activity is too big, think of ways to break it into smaller jobs.

14 Opportunities to raise money are all around you. Pay attention.

15 Keep trying, especially when an activity or team meeting doesn't go exactly as planned.

16 If you are representing an organisation, remember that your actions reflect on their group.

17 You are in good company as a fundraiser because giving is on the rise! According to the organisation Charity Facts, there are about 170,000 charities in England and Wales.

18 Get involved at many levels and in different ways. This will teach you new things.

19 Think about putting aside some money weekly or monthly to help others.

20 Work hard and have fun!

Further Information

You can find out more about raising money by looking at websites and books. Many charity organisations list ideas for fundraising activities for children and teens. Here are some helpful places to start.

Websites

www.unicef.org/voy/
The UNICEF Youth Voice website provides suggestions for fundraisers, guidelines, success stories from around the world, fundraising packets, and even an interactive online fundraising folder.

www.worldwildlife.org
The World Wildlife Fund is the world's largest wildlife conservation organisation. The charity operates worldwide to protect natural areas and wild animals, including endangered species.

www.savethechildren.org
The Save the Children website tells people how to get involved with kids' art contests, e-cards, and more.

www.wish.org
The Make-a-Wish Foundation is an international organisation that helps seriously ill children by making their dreams come true. It began in the United States and now operates in more than 30 countries around the world.

www.justgive.org.uk
The JustGive site lists UK charities and UK charities events. You can also post your own charity event on this site.

www.rspcavic.org/kids_stuff
The Royal Society for the Prevention of Cruelty to Animals (RSPCA) was founded in 1824, which makes it one of the oldest animal welfare charities in the world. It is also one of the largest charities in the UK, and is funded by voluntary donations.

www.nspcc.org.uk/GetInvolved/
The website of the National Society for the Prevention of Cruelty to Children has many ideas and resources for fundraising in schools.

www.rednoseday.com
This website discusses Red Nose Day and lists fast fundraising ideas. It also includes success stories about school events.

BOOKS

Teach Yourself Fundraising, Jenny Barlow (Teach Yourself Books, 2002)

World Organizations: International Red Cross, Kathleen Prior and Ralf Perkins (Franklin Watts, 2001)

Money: Fund-Raising, Julie Haydon (Smart Apple Media, 2006)

Some International Charity Campaigns

In The Pink

Pink is the adopted colour of the Breast Cancer Care organisation. As part of Breast Cancer Awareness Month (each October), people are invited to hold "pink" events to raise money for people affected by breast cancer. Suggested activites include holding pink parties with pink food and drinks, and running pink quizzes at schools and colleges – with pink prizes, of course!

Knit One Save One

Did you know that knitting a hat for a newborn baby can help to save its life? Because a newborn baby cannot regulate its body temperature, it is more likely to develop diseases such as pneumonia. This serious illness kills an estimated two million babies every year. The children's charity, Save the Children, has launched a campaign asking people to knit hats for newborn babies around the world. Log on to their website on **www.savethechildren.org.uk** to find out more.

Glossary

agenda matters to be dealt with in a particular order, usually on a list

amenity anything that adds to comfort or convenience, such as toilets, heating, or running water

chairperson person who heads a meeting

charity organisation that helps those in need

chronic continuous, present all the time

chronological arranged in order of time

committee group that represents, or makes decisions for, a larger group or organisation

contract formal agreement made between two or more people

division of labour act of breaking down a large job into smaller ones

donate give something away for free

flat fee fixed amount of payment

flyer written announcement

genuine real or true

improvise do something without any preparation

letter campaign effort to raise money by sending out letters to potential donors

licence written official permission to hold an activity

merchandise products associated with a charity that are sold to raise funds

minutes official record of what is said at a meeting

mission purpose or aim

permit document that gives you formal or legal permission to do or use something

pledge promise to give money once a certain task is completed

press release letter sent to local media organisations, such as newspapers and television stations

proceeds money earned from a fundraising activity

publicity advertising that will bring something to public attention

raffle activity in which a person pays for the opportunity to win a prize

secretary person who keeps records, and writes letters on behalf of an organisation or committee

sponsor supporter who pays
money to help a cause or
organisation

takings money received by selling
goods or fundraising

treasurer person on a committee
who is in charge of the money

vendor supplier

waiver agree to give up
something

Index